Odyssey of Love:
A Poetry Collection
By Joseph C. Reyes

© Copyright 2021

Table of Contents

Identity and Life..

   Identity..

   Work of Art..

   Life is..

   Thankful..

   Poetry Made Me Realize.....

   When I Look at Me.....

   Phoenix Rising..

   Midlife Crisis..

   The Day I Accepted Myself..

   Friday of Freedom..

   Seasons of Hope..

   Duality..

   Future..

Love..

   Cosmic Love..

   Scarlet Woman..

   Goddess..

   Your Love..

   My Sun and Moon..

   The Love I Long For..

That Precious Gift 23

Ode to Your Love...24

Tell Me Your Secrets 25

Young Love...26

Northern Lights 27

Invisible Love 28

Apricot Hued Skies 29

My Broken Pieces 30

Sun That Never Sets...31

Wished Upon a Snowflake..................................32

Lost 33

My Joy 34

Your Cure, Your Love, Your Light 35

Ramblings of The Heart 36

Camera 38

My Guidance 39

Here I Am 40

I'm Yours 41

The Magic of True Love 42

Eternally Poetically Yours...................................43

Show Me the Road...44

Crime of Love 45

Pretty Words...46

Let Me Fall 47

If Love Had an Address 48

Forbidden Fruit 49

Things I Love to Think About 50

December Love 51

Heartbreak 53

Why Wasn't It Me? 54

Talking to The Moon 55

Scars 56

Looking Out the Window 57

Paperback Writer 58

Oxygen 59

Windswept Moments 60

Winter 61

Expectations 62

Memories 63

Years Have Gone by 64

Think About You 66

Broken Dreams 67

Faded Memory 68

Broken Promises 69

Puppet Master 70

Broken Heart 71

Love Dies 72

The One 73

Story of Us 74

Words of Sentiment 76

No Longer Us 77

Foolish 78

I've Paid 79

Free Falling 80

You and Me 81

You Don't Know Me 82

My Favorites 83

With Time 84

Artificial Relief 85

Travel in Time 86

Hard to Say I'm Sorry. 87

Poisoned Love 88

Healing 89

Angel, Rest in Peace 90

Depression 92

I Was Born 93

Ghosts of The Past 94

Tonight 95

I Didn't Ask You To... 96

Bound by Bones 97

Incapable 98

Bilingual Poetry 101

Llévame 102

Take Me 103

Amor Encerrado 104

Lockdown Love 105

Èchame La Culpa 106

Blame Me 107

Girasol 108

Sunflower 109

Rosas de Amor 110

Roses of Love 111

Sombra de Amor 112

Shade of Love 113

Estrellas fugaces 114

Falling stars 115

Amor de Madre 116

A Mother's Love 117

Renacido 118

Reborn 119

Fortaleza 120

Stronghold 121

Note to Readers 123

Odyssey of Love • Joseph C. Reyes

Odyssey of Love • Joseph C. Reyes

Identity and Life

Identity

I hide behind a mask of skin and bones,
without much substance or colorful tones…
or that's what people see I suppose.

I am much kinder underneath,
much more than what people perceive.
Why don't people want to get to know me?
Must it be because they're afraid of me?

The truth of the matter is that
none of that is true.
People are too shallow
to even get close to me.
No one has the decency
to know the real me.

But the end of it all is:
I don't care what people think of me,
my real friends are the ones that believe in me,
and I know I finally have my own identity.

Work of Art

I am on a path that only I can control.
Life paints blackness into my soul,
that I cover with a smile day by day.
I may seem blank and empty under it all,
but I am full of color.
Don't judge for what you see,
dig deep and discover
what is blind to the naked eye.

In the end,
you will know,
I am a work of art.

Life is...

Life is a damaged boat
sailing along placid waves,
traveling lost through endless sea
discovering unimaginable things.
Guided by wondrous stars in the night sky,
I journey to a destination untold.
I'm awakened by a dreadful storm,
it tries to throw me overboard.
But I will not let it shake me,
I have more crusades
yet to cease and conquer.

Thankful

Today I feel anew,
I am finally feeling not so blue.
Though this year has been really hard,
I am very thankful I have come this far.
In this arena of humanity,
I've fought many battles
and keep claiming victory.
Although my health has been pretty bad,
I am thankful for the family I have.
I was on the verge of sudden death,
but God gave me the will and breath.
All my friends have been a gift,
my view on this will always persist.
This is why I rather be kind,
it's my way of having peace of mind.
Cheers to those who are reading this,
I hope you find nothing but comfort and bliss.
And though this year is not at its end,
I look forward to the next year ahead.

Poetry Made Me Realize...

Poetry made me realize how much I had to say,
that I shouldn't store this pain away.

I write only because
there is a voice within that cannot be sustained.

My heart overflows
with wonderful expressions
of love, friendship and
the fruits bared in this life.

I am pressed to write my feelings before I expire.
I cannot contain these words any longer.

I pen these thoughts without a care.
These dreams and emotions I want to share.

When I Look at Me...

When I look at me,
I see not what you see.
When I look at me,
I don't see myself blindly,
I do so truthfully.
When I look at me
I see a young man with a brave heart,
who did it, even often hid it.
When I look at me,
when I *really* look at me,
I smile and wish you too could see,
My soul staring back,
gleamingly.

Phoenix Rising

My greatest weakness
is my greatest strength
My heart burns with great intensity.
The fire burns hard...
Flames from yellow to orange,
blushing and gushing.
It burns,
like a volcano,
whenever my outpouring face
in the mirror I see.
I hate how people look at me.
My heart burns astoundingly...
that's exactly why my mind turns against me.
Weakness becomes strength again.
I fall quick, but,
I always rise again,
with perseverance flowing through my veins.
Remember what a strong man I've been.
Do not waste my generosity.

After all these brandings,
you'll watch this Phoenix
rising from the ashes.

Midlife Crisis

There are times I have no idea what to write.
I hate trying to force my feelings on this page,
often at late hours of the night.
Should I be pondering the meaning of life?
I rather let these thoughts flow onto my notes
and watch a beautiful creation of verses unfold.

I waste my time
picking and choosing
stories of my past I'd rather lose.
There's no use in pouting about my sad life,
or the things that make me cry myself to sleep
every other night.
I need to live for the now,
not the things that should or might
happen in the coming days
or subsequent years.
Those will only cause stress and fears.

My life will now change.
I won't let my past hurt me again.
I choose to be happy
and be proud of being me.

The Day I Accepted Myself ...

The day I accepted myself,
I knew I was never meant to be
your Prince Charming,
a dazzling knight in shining armor,
meant to save you.

You didn't need to be saved.
I needed to save myself from you.

Like a venomous snake,
striking for the hunt,
I was seduced by your sweet words
that became lethal to my heart.

But my soul knew better.
It quickly rescued me from your deadly grasp.

I knew I didn't need you to be happy
because,
the day I accepted myself,
I didn't care what you thought of me anymore.

I finally knew what I was worth.
I knew what I deserved.
And I knew that it wasn't
You

Friday of Freedom

It's Friday afternoon
and I don't know what to do.
It's the start of newfound freedom,
for most,
yet, I shrug in bed
pondering my dreams and aspirations.
Though I feel empty inside,
I know I can reach great heights.
I may not know what I want now,
But I know,
my Friday of freedom
is in reach,
somewhere in the clouds.

Seasons of Hope

My mind wrestles with frost-bitten thoughts,
even my heart has turned into winter frost.

But I forgot the seasons change,
when Spring comes
and everything around me turns green again.
My heart begins to race;
enthusiasm runs through my veins,
even in Spring sometimes it rains.
Moving towards Summer
with the oceans so deep as neverland,
my heart fills with overwhelming joy and laughter.
But with yellow Autumn and a warmer heart
these rhymes will end.

I turned back to Winter and suddenly realized,
the cold was only pretend.

Duality

It's time I expose your
vexatious duality,
the two-faced lies you have
been constantly denying.
I cannot fix your double personality.
The mask you wear is a blindfold,
closing you off to reality.

You are a pleasant friend by day,
but a ghastly monster at night.
You are the Dr. Jekyll and Mr. Hyde of life,
you should be ashamed of the things
you desperately try to hide.

I'd like to see the day you finally change,
but it's on you to take the initiative.
So, take off the blindfold,
and open your eyes
to the love within your heart,
and I promise,
your mind will always
have peaceful thoughts.

Future

What does the future
hold for me?
I hope it's what I dream of
in my sleep.
The things we see in movies and tv
are the things of vanity.
Money, fame and fortune
are the things people seek.
True love, health and family
are worth more to uncovering.
Like slaying dragons
and dissolving evil spells,
life can give lots of living hell.
It's not the stuff of fairy tales
and happily ever afters,
it's about the things
that truly ever matter.

Odyssey of Love • Joseph C. Reyes

Love

Cosmic Love

The heavens proclaim
my love for you,
The stars twinkling at night
as bright as your eyes.
Even in a storm
my love never trembles,
for at its end,
the clouds depart,
revealing a beautiful rainbow
waiting to rise
from the evergreen moss.
I want to endeavor endlessly
in the cosmos of mysteries
that is your soul,
letting them collide
like shooting stars,
forever becoming one supernovic world.

Scarlet Woman

A woman
doesn't need a man
to achieve happiness.
She's resilient and brave.
Life has taught her
the world is cruel and mean.
But she reflects strength,
avoiding mistakes of the past.
She's tender, soft hearted.
This scarlet woman embodies
beauty, love and respect.

Goddess

You are a goddess,
walking amongst humanity.
Your beauty is perceived by many,
it makes the moon shine with jealousy.
Your voice is sweet,
like the sea breeze.
Your smile is a marvel,
shining brighter than the sun.
Your eyes sparkle and twinkle,
it makes the stars gaze in wonder.
You are a goddess,
and one day I hope to be your god.

Your Love

Your love is a sharp edge,
piercing through this bleeding heart.
The cure for this aching pain
is the sight of your beautiful smile
And the sound of the sweet song
That is your voice.

My Sun and Moon

Your smile brightens my day like the sunlight,
    your eyes twinkle like the stars under the moonlit sky.
Your embrace is warmer than the sun's rays,
    it moves me like the moon moves the waves.
You brighten my mood as the sun fills the sky,
    my soul goes dark as the night when you say goodbye.
Please don't leave me when the day has past,
    promise to come back before the moon
    names the last star tonight.

The Love I Long For

Every night I dream of you,
feeling comfort in your warm embrace.
I long for your love every day,
when I see your face
in the clouds hugging the sky.
When my soul feels black and white,
thinking of you fills my day
with colors so bright.
As my broken heart burns in fire,
nature reminds of your beauty.
I can't wait for that first morning,
finally waking up in your arms,
from dreams of your loving.

That Precious Gift

Life denies me your presence,
I only see you in my dreams.
With every passing day,
my mind wants to taste your lips.

Your face is reflected on the moon,
your smile sparkles in the stars.

I hear your voice as a silent whisper,
hiding in the wind.

I smell you in the flowers,
your fragrance envelops my being.

I feel emptiness inside me,
a loneliness I cannot keep
from Lady Agony.

I crave to hold you closer,
forever on my shoulder,
kissing your neck.

Your love is that precious gift
I pray and long for.

Ode to Your Love

Our shadows intertwined
under the sunlight,
our souls shine so bright.
I dream of you every night,
wishing for your tantalizing touch
under the moonlit sky.
I ache to be in your arms,
holding me close when it's dark.
I crave the taste of your lips,
that sweet flavor of love and bliss.
Your beauty and splendor,
not to be withheld.
Nothing will ever compare.

Tell Me Your Secrets

Show me who you are,
Your delicate intricacies,
        your pleasures,
           your dreams,
              your aspirations,
the passion glowing from your voluptuous skin,
the treasures you keep hidden in the clouds.

Tell me your secrets,
what you want, what you desire,
what the moon whispers
to your ears at the wake of night.

Let me penetrate your dark side,
your temptations, your fantasies,
the nightmares that wake you up
in the early hours of the morning.
Expose yourself to me,
unveil the deepest parts of your complexities.
Take me into your deepest thoughts,
the happiest moments, the saddest stories,
the ones haunting your mind.
Don't be ashamed or scared,
because from now and forever,
my heart will be haven to your secrets and prayers.

Young Love

My heart beats at a fast pace.
Your beauty turns heads
in the hallway.
I stare at your beautiful eyes,
wondering if you see the love in my soul
or just the blunder of crashing against a pole.
Everyone laughs,
but your soft hands soothe the pain.
What did I do to deserve such sweetness?
When the world hates me
but you pay no attention to my limits?
I thought I had a chance with you,
daydreaming about the things we could do.
Showing all the ways my heart longs for you.

Only,
my love was lost in desperation.
My eyes only saw perfection,
and my heart broke for the first time
with your rejection.

Northern Lights

Northern lights shining bright,
your magnificence shown in the summer night.
Let love and beauty illuminate the sky tonight.
Your movements make me reminisce of our dance,
gifting peace on those
who stare upon your elegance.
I hear your voice in the wind,
a whistling whisper of tinted truths
in the glow of darkness.
You dance around the lustful moon,
teasing your perfect curves
around the staring stars.
Even when I feel dark deep inside,
your gaze always fills me with its light.

Invisible Love

I dream about her all night
It's silly to think about really,
I don't even know this angelic being,
flawless in my head.
I can only see her beaming soul
illuminating my dreams.
She is love pure and perfection.
Her rebellious personality
pulls me in with magnetic intention.
I don't know her face,
I don't know her appearance,
I just know this obvious attraction
to her is true.

I know,
I want to spend eternity with her.

Apricot Hued Skies

Dancing under apricot hued skies
I look deep into your crystal blue eyes,
inhaling your beauty,
filling my bones with overwhelming ecstasy.
I crave the first kiss
from those sweet lips.
The sound of your voice
is a sweet elixir whispering in my ear.
We have desired this love for so long,
but cold our souls have been.
I want to dwell
in the Winter Wonderland of your heart
where a nightmarish blizzard
has turned into a beautiful snowfall.
I wish to wipe your tears
away from your face,
holding you forever in my arms,
feeling this beautiful heartfelt bliss,
loving you incessantly
in the warmth of your embrace.

My Broken Pieces

You picked up my broken pieces
and put me back together,
puzzle pieces hidden in each star.
Your kind words
healed my wounded heart.
Like a calming balm,
Your smile
soothed my bleeding scars.
The touch of your soft hands
wiped my tears away.
Words cannot express
how much I feel blessed
to have you as my everlasting friend.

Sun That Never Sets

My heart
will speak what I could never say,
my love for you is never dead.
My soul
has anchored itself to my devotion for you;
my life feels empty and meaningless without you.
Deep in the chambers of this kindred heart,
burns an eternal warmth for you.
My love is always pure,
because not even death
my love can remove.

I wish for you
to be the everlasting roof over my head,
and in return,
I'll be your sun that never sets.

Wished Upon a Snowflake

She wished upon a sparkling snowflake,
wishing for a true love to meet.
Before the snowflake melted,
she looked into my eyes,
and she knew that her wish
had always been me.

Lost

I feel lost in this world of pain,
sad and lonely,
in a battle with my brain.
A love like you I yearn for,
it makes my heart ache.
I have looked for you endlessly,
but my efforts have been in vain.

I wonder if you've travelled the world,
looking for me in every country,
every city
every state.
Where can I find you?
Please tell me.
I would travel the seven seas,
if you would only meet with me.
Is it that you need saving?
Because for you,
I would do anything.
I wish to reach your heart
and be safe forever in your arms.
I am eager to show you my love,
promising to be with you until death do us part,
even for eternity.

My Joy

I wished so many times I was with you,
the one for which my love is pure.
I don't care where we are or what we do,
my life,
    my love,
        my joy,
comes from being with you.

Your Cure, Your Love, Your Light

I know you think you're drowning,
my soul can feel you're afraid.
I promise things will get better,
my love is yours until the very end.

I will touch wherever you hurt
and cure your bleeding scars.
I just want to make you happy,
making endless memories with you instead.
I will be your healer with my love,
and make sure you always feel safe.

This love I feel is pure and real,
my heart beats in endless bliss.
So, take my hand and hold it tight,
I will forever be your guiding light.
Please don't ever leave my side,
for you will always have a place in my life,
until the day comes
when God tells me,
"It's time to say goodbye."

Ramblings of The Heart

I know a little something
about what you're feeling right now.
You're giving off all the signs,
                    the tells,
                          the vibes.
I know you better than you wish to know.
You think you can play mind games with me,
distracting me from your deepest thoughts?
I invented those tricks mister.
I have waited long enough for you to admit it.
The way you gaze at her,
the way your eyes twitch,
the silly giggle,
the stuttering of your words...
                    they all scream it out loud!
But your mouth won't say it.
You're afraid of the what ifs, the buts, the could be's,
your own insecurities,
and worst of all, the pain...
the pain of having me broken
into a million teeny, tiny pieces.

Well, there's one little thing
I won't let you live with
                    -- regret.

Because what you're feeling,
maybe for the first time in forever,
is such a beautiful pure thing.
And this time, it is real.
Not something you are imagining,
hallucinating or
dreaming about.
This,
my friend,
is True Love.

Camera

I always bring my camera with me,
taking pictures of everything.
You might think I'm a little crazy,
maybe a little annoying,
but you'll soon understand
what I'm doing.

The images of us are the best ones,
even after death
these will stay as lasting memories.
Our minds archive
the best and worst thoughts,
but this camera will capture
the beautiful story of us.

Let the film settle in,
for this love of ours
was always meant to be.
Forever and always,
we'll become a long-lasting relationship,
captured in film,
drawn in the stars.

My Guidance

If only you could be my North Star,
guiding me in the right direction
towards happiness.
Should I turn left,   or maybe right,
                or just straightforward,
towards your shining light?
You are the one that makes my life so bright,
the one that always sees beauty in my soul
even when I don't feel right.

If only you were my compass,
just for one night,
would you show me the way towards a joyful life?
Help me learn my life's purpose,
pull me out of this despairing sea
of endless tears.
I have no enthusiasm to live any longer,
if it's at the hands of solitude
that my fate has wandered.
The only one
who gives meaning to my life is you.
The only one
I have ever truly loved is you,
it's always been and always will be you.

Here I Am

Here I am
talking to myself again,

watching your favorite movie
on rewind,

listening to your favorite song
on loop…

Yet, I wish I knew,
do you love me,
as much as I love you?

There's nothing more
that I want or need.
This love I feel has engulfed me
like a fire burning on a tree.
Don't let these feelings die in vain
I will love and care for you
until the very end.

I'm Yours

I have found you to be a precious treasure.
Your love is more valuable
than any gem
and more abundant
than all the money
this world could ever hold.

You have found true love in me,
there's nothing better
than being in your company.
I give you the keys
to my heart and soul,
a kingdom for you to explore.
Leave no box unopened,
              no stone unturned.

I know our love will never die,
as long as we stay together,
our love laced with gold
and endless time.

The Magic of True Love

I do believe magic exists,
but not in the sense
magicians do their tricks.
Love can come out of nowhere
And just as easily
disappear
into thin air.
Love is not
meant to be picked out of a hat,
or like sawing yourself in half
and expecting it to last.
Only true love
is meant to last forever.
Love is the bonding of two hearts
transforming into one.

THAT

is the most
magical of things there will ever be.

Eternally Poetically Yours

Words don't mean anything
if they don't come with actions,
they say.
But what do I do,
when you're so far away
and words are all I have to display?
While I try to free myself
from this drunken stupor of love,
　　　　　my heart,
　　　　　　　　oh my heart
speaks f r e e l y of the wonders
of what could be and what might be.
You might think I'm crazy,
And I would say
"That's too small of a word,"
for you have no idea
I would move mountains just to hold you.
But I know too well I cannot have you,
I cannot be with you but
it's when my heart speaks
through these words that I can only dream
and be
Eternally, Poetically
Yours.

Show Me the Road

Show me the road to you,
because lost I am without you.
Teach me how to win your heart,
for I can no longer breathe
if I can't be with you.
Guide me to everlasting bliss,
where our eyes will meet
for our first kiss.
Let me wipe your tears away and
fill the cracks and scars in your soul
with the love you so much deserve.
I will follow your lead,
because my heart and soul are yours
from now to eternity.

Crime of Love

You turn heads
everywhere you go.
Men envy that soul of yours.
But they cannot have
what is not yours to let go,
because little do they know
your heart will soon be
in my palms.
For I will have committed
the biggest heist
in the history of love:
I will have stolen your golden heart.
I will be your joy,
    your peace,
      your home,
your one and only
Criminal of Love.

Pretty Words

I do not need pretty words
to invoke the love
my heart contains.
I gaze up at the stars,
watch them trace your name,
hoping they align one day
to include mine by your side.
The heavens testify
of my melancholy and constant pain,
because for your love
I still yearn for every day.

Let Me Fall

Let me fall for you,
even if you don't feel the same way.
Let me hold you,
maybe just once,
even if it ends in pain.
I'd rather have loved you,
than have lived without telling you.

If Love Had an Address

If love had an address,
I would search far and wide
to be with you.
Knocking on every door,
looking in every window pane
for your face,
no obstacle is big enough
to get in the way,
for my love is deep and true.
Open the lock to your heart
and I promise,
you won't have regrets,
because now I know
I have found a peaceful home,

in you.

Forbidden Fruit

I have this aching temptation
to be with you
that I will never shake.
I have spent many nights
fantasizing about us.
Stargazing under the moonlight,
my knees growing weak
at the thought
of stealing a kiss from you.

But I know too well
of the possibility,
often in deniability,
we are never meant to be.
It's only but a dream
to enjoy the pleasures
of this forbidden tree,
And turning its fruits
into an eternal sin.

Things I Love to Think About

I think about the vast universe
and it's infinite number of stars;
How the world revolves around the sun,
providing light and heat selflessly;
How the moon shines her light
above the ocean waves.
I think about how much I love chocolate,
I'm just a sucker for intricate sweets.
But the best part is,
all these things make me think of YOU.

You are my universe,
the only one I can ever belong to.
You are my world,
my life revolves only around you.
You are my sun and my moon,
you brighten the darkest parts of my life
and warm my heart.
You are my chocolate,
the one who's words
are always genuine and sweet.

You are the only one on my mind,
the reason why my love will never weaken.

December Love

My heart beats to the rhythm of your love,
souls intertwined,
charmed by the tender twinkles of your eyes.
Your voice entangles me
amongst whispered wishes,
feeling like a December dream in your arms.

What the world looks like without you,
I have no clue,
for you are my entire universe.

I hope this love never dies;
with you, I want to be with,
for a thousand lives.

Odyssey of Love • Joseph C. Reyes

Heartbreak

Why Wasn't It Me?

Why wasn't it me,
the one you called
when you needed someone there,
for an ear to be lent,
a shoulder to cry on?
I always wanted you to look at me,
make you see the love I had to give.
But that was of zero worth,
I was nothing but an invisible ghost.
You were the popular girl
hanging with the jocks,
I,
the quiet one
sitting in the corner,
     alone,

      shy,

      with the undesirable quirks.

Why wasn't it me?
Maybe it was,
I just wasn't there to see.

Talking to The Moon

I talk to the moon every night.
She speaks of the stars passing by,
and I can't help but tell her,
they remind me
of you and I, and the love
we once had.
She responds
with the beautiful melodies
of the night,
and all I can do is cry,
knowing I don't have you by my side,
realizing that our love has passed.
I tell her,
I'm willing to give anything and everything,
for a chance to hear
your voice one more time.

She smiles and says,
"It's best to let go.
Your love is always there,
written for eternity,
in your dreams."

Scars

These are words I longed to say,
I just didn't know how to explain.
Your name was sewn to my heart,
until your rejection pulled it apart.
Your words cut me deep,
they made my veins bleed.
Your memory burns like fire,
slowly incinerating my insides.
The sound of your voice
makes me inconsolable,
suffocating in tears at night.
I trusted you with my heart,
and you tore it to shards.
I thought my scars had healed,
but the scabs opened with your return.
My mind goes crazy with the pain you've caused,
but now I think it's time to move on.
I write these words not to say goodbye,
this is just for my peace of mind.

Looking Out the Window

I still look out the window,
thinking about what could have been.
Watching the rain fall down,
my tears start flowing out.
My heart of glass shatters into pieces,
Driven by insanity.
You took off without a hint.
No sign left of your stay with me.
All I have is your memory.

Paperback Writer

I want to be a paperback writer,
scribbling through the pages of time.
My heart is set on these poetic verses,
hoping to come upon love in this hateful life.
My pages keep turning,
ink smudging,
painful memories haunting my mind.
My soul stings with dreadful disappointment,
yet, my thoughts are always clinging
on the hopes my luck changes one day.

Oxygen

I thought I could live without you
Only you felt like oxygen to my brain
feeling like a love I could not sustain.
I inhaled your words,
but they poisoned my lungs instead.
You hurt my soul with treachery,
making me bleed profusely.
I believed your sweet lies,
Yet they were nothing but
a wolf in disguise.
But if this is love,
I'd rather keep dreaming
than be caught dead
in your trap.

Windswept Moments

Within the windswept moments of time,
your memory has slipped away
with the bitter taste of red wine.

Your departure has left me to insanity,
singing love songs
in a state of drunken melancholy.

You were my one and only muse,
the one I would always choose.

I got lost between the sands of your soul,
but your two-faced lies wilted our love
like a flower planted in the dust.

What was the last touch like before you let go,
when your gift of presence
was all I had ever known?

You made me forget,
 you left me in the streets for dead,
disregarding the three words I ever said:

I love you

Winter

Who will take winter from my heart,
this freezing iceburg in my soul,
when I have no one
in my life to love and hold?

I want to reach for the sky,
from the morning until the sunset
reaches her eyes,
because without her love
I simply cannot survive.

Gravity pulls me back
to my somber reality.
My bed sheets have been soaked
with tears of agony,
my life crumbling at the hands of Aphrodite.

Even so,
I will wait for her to find me.
I will not despair and lose sanity.
I am full of hope and desire
because I know my day will come
when I will be with her for eternity.

Expectations

I have been rendered speechless.
Freedom from you
has given me peace and rest.
This magic spell has broken.
My aching heart will never be frozen.
I have placed a wall there
so no one will touch it
Tears in my eyes won't come again,
for a drop of love, you never gave.
I'm sick of your little masquerade.
I won't talk about feeling numb inside,
I have nowhere else to hide,
but these lines I have to write.
Why must I let you play with my mind?
I won't let you steal my breath away
and persistently hope my pain will end.
For, now I can live with less expectation,
and cut you from this useless equation

Until the last thing I have to say is,
"Farewell,
Don't even beg to stay."

Memories

You saw darkness in your eyes,
those days you felt pain inside.
But only I saw beauty and light,
where the stars twinkle
and the moon shines
in the winter night.

You were
     my love,
          my dream,
               my obsession.
The one
I could never beg to stay.

But our love was written in the sand;
you let it die without affection.
If it had been written in stone
it would have survived.

Now memories of you are all I have.

Odyssey of Love • Joseph C. Reyes

Years Have Gone by

Your heart was never mine and
though you gave it away,
without thought,
these words I longed to say:

You are a beautiful flower,
making love bloom freely
and making my soul everglow
at the sight of your electric smile.

People think I've gone mad,
just because
I feel this love I've always had.
They will never understand,
this ardent love will never subside.
My loyalty you will always have.

But years have gone by
and I still don't understand
why I don't have you by my side.
There's not one second in my life
you're not on my mind.

I love you
even if I have to wait for you
for eternity,
or die,
and be with you in another life

Think About You

I think about you all the time,
sometimes with tears
running from my eyes,
wondering if you
dream of me at your bedside.

I think about your glowing gaze,
the one the stars can't even replicate.
One look into your profound eyes
and this heart of mine
flutters with delight.

Do you even care what I feel inside,
that you are the one
that makes my soul so bright?

For, you are my star that gives me light,
the only one I want to be with
for the rest of my life.

Broken Dreams

I'm tangled in a menacing cobweb
of broken dreams,
each one weaved bigger than me.
My life has become an awful infestation
of fears and expectations.
My heart knows I can't live like this,
it clings on hope
that there is good hidden in me,
even if I'm not able to perceive.
Yet, fate knows things
will turn around for me;
a love like no other
I will soon receive
and finally, the love of my life
will always be with me.

For,
just as the night turns into day,
happiness will shine inside me again.

Faded Memory

It wasn't easy to realize
you weren't the one for me.
My mind spins in circles
thinking of why you had to leave me,
tearing my heart into a million pieces.

I ink these words
with hopes
you will read them one day,
because it's all I have left to say.
I know now I've become an afterthought.
This embodiment of a poet just lacks one thing—

Your everlasting love for me.

But one day without me
is all you needed to make me a faded memory.

And you were just a dissolving
d
r
e
a
m.

Broken Promises

You filled my life with broken promises,
tinseled snippets of who you would be,
and I fell victim to those
soft-spoken instances.
You chose to spit on words
you couldn't keep,
yet I'm the one
who has to live with this painful agony.

You live like a princess in distress,
playing the prisoner,
I must confess.
But I will not fall for your deceit,
I won't let you make a fool out of me.
I would rather live desolately
than deal with your dishonesty.

If you wish to come back to me,
come for a visit when I'm six feet deep.
I'd like to see if you have the audacity
to apologize when I'm deceased.

Puppet Master

My life revolved around you.
My axis of solitude
geared around you,
My Moon.

Your happiness is all I cared for.
You took advantage
and in the process
I lost sight of who I was.
planet or puppet, thereof.
Your manipulation
is no longer tolerated.
I need to cut the strings
on my back
and set myself free.
I'm done falling a victim
of your puppeteering.

Broken Heart

I'm picking up the pieces
of my broken heart,
healing from old wounds
and new scars.
I know I will stop bleeding
soon enough,
and let love back
into my weakening heart.

Love can cure all things,
I have to believe,
and fill this empty void inside of me.
I don't want any part-time love
that others have given me,
those guilty pleasures are now the old me.
My soul will spring for new pleasantries,
where life has new meaning
and true love will reign free.

But for now,
the heart waits, wounded, patiently.

Love Dies

There is no such thing as hope,
It dies in the woods,
dressed in flames.
There is no use in waiting,
it's just torture in vain.
Souls will never connect,
misconstrued pieces lost in space.
There's nothing on the other side,
a wall never meant to collapse.
There is only hurt and pain,
Because after all this time,
love dies in the end.

The One

I am lost in my feelings for you,
My heart doesn't want to accept the truth.
    The torture,
        the pain,
            the anguish,
I just cannot, will not take it!
I am madly in love with you,
no one else matters more than you.
I put you on a pedestal,
the most perfect amongst God's creations.
If only you knew,
how deeply I'm falling for you.
I would probably let all my bones break
from the simplest thought of you.
But this I know is true,
my soul is broken because I can't have you.
I have to accept
I'm just not "The One" for you.

Story of Us

People have asked me
about the story of us,
but the reality is
there hardly was such a thing as "us".
I could make up
an unabridged version of our time,
but I really don't want
to lie and sound obnoxious.
Don't get me wrong,
I loved you and all,
but what's the point
if you never made an effort?
I could fill books
with my thoughts of you,
but that's the last thing
I ever want to do,
when it's all
pain and sorrow,
to the point I want to pull my brain
and make my skull hollow.

So, I've come to terms with a solution:
I'll handle talking about you,
and whatever it is we were,
even if I have to do it
through gritting teeth,
just as long as you stay away from me.

Words of Sentiment

I spill these words of sentiment
that I dare not convey,
but I do not, cannot
just throw away.
My tears speak volumes of
the things my mouth cannot say,
and the past that drowns me,
S l o w l y,
    p a i n f u l l y
                day by day.
I write to mend the rift in my broken heart,
but things feel the same,
I'm sorry to say.
I wish I could translate my words
to the strength my friends think I possess,
but my pen stays paralyzed,
unless I bleed out words
of sadness and pain.

No Longer Us

There is you.
There is me.
No longer us.
Just two birds,
uncaged,
set free.
And yet,
my heart called out to you,
begging you to stay,
along with tears
expressing words
my mouth could never say.
The joy I felt being with you
has now faded away.
The fire of love
that burned in my heart for so long
has been extinguished,
leaving nothing left
but dark fumes of painful memories.

Foolish

I was foolish
to believe in love.
My heart has been broken
into a million bloody parts.
When will this suffering ever end?
You stabbed my heart
and pulled it apart.
You laughed and enjoyed my pain,
While I lay there bleeding in vain.
But I was too good for you,
Perhaps, my kind words
were not enough for you.
Now there is nothing more I want to do,
but to die in a dismal graveyard,
than live with the thought of you;
and quit on love for good.

I've Paid

It was effortless,
effortless the way
I saw you slowly slip away,
away from my heart
and out of my sight,
the sight of you
that once made me smile
but now just a memory
that makes me cry myself
to sleep at night,
nights that end in dreams
of grief and pain,
pain that you handed me freely
for the love I had to give,

but I guess that's how life
has me pay for the mistakes
I've made.

Free Falling

You hit me with your arrow
of so-called love,
Unaware that you laced it
with poison at its tip.
You dragged me
with your sugar-coated lies
before I could realize
the fatal blow had really set in,
falling hard and fast on feelings
that we were meant to be.
Now I find myself
f
r
e
e
f
a
l
l
i
n
g
in a bottomless abyss
at the hands of your torture and treachery.

You and Me

You and me
was all I could see,
along the beach,
in the waves made by seas of green.
For so long all I've wanted,
is a day in your arms
than a million without your soft touch.
A day in your presence
is like living in a garden of roses,
and now all I crave
is one more moment
in your delicate fragrance.

You Don't Know Me

You don't know me,
    the real me,
        the feelings I hold deep,
            the secrets that I keep,
just so you stay close to me.
But I'm rapidly growing weak,
holding back tears,
my heart growing unbearably heavy,
for this love I feel,
a love that will never be returned,
and my life ending in despair.

My Favorites

My favorites were those poems
that I wrote to you at night,
those that made me smile
when I saw you
for the first time,
those that made me think
of your amazing laughter.
But now I know
forever isn't meant to last.
All I have are lines
of things left unsaid
and a million reasons
why I want to cry.

With Time

With time I will understand
that life is sometimes sad,
but it's not meant to last.
With time I will understand,
the mistakes I've made
have driven you away.
With time I will understand
we weren't meant to be,
our love was a fictional fantasy.
With time I will understand,
this pain will eventually dissipate,
my heart will learn to love again.

Artificial Relief

Who can really make my day,
and take this aching pain away?

It's not like I can say:
"Hey Siri,
don't take this as a selfish plea,
but will you bring my love to me?"

Nor can I make this request:
"Alexa,
rescue me from this sorrow
and dry my tears away"

For no artificial intelligence
can ever yank away this love for you
and stop the yearning I have to be with you.

Travel in Time

I wish I could go back,
back in time
into the vortex of past memories,
to find the love I never told,
to mend the mistakes I sorely regret,
to tell her, I love her, once more,
to make sure our future
is set in stone,
and our happiness lasts
tomorrow and forevermore.

Hard to Say I'm Sorry.

I've made mistakes
that I cannot erase,
and said things
I'm not proud of expelling.
Which makes this
much harder to say,
how sorry I am for my disdain.
I don't know
if things will ever change,
and if you'll ever think of me
or miss me.
I'm sorry my ego
got in the way,
I never intended
to hurt you this way.
All I wish is for you to stay safe,
so, it's best for us to part ways.
And I truly hope one day
you'll find happiness again.

Poisoned Love

You try to sway her,
seduce her,
deceive her,
with your honey-glazed words
that are nothing but poisonous lies.
You say you never want to hurt her,
but you turn around and stab her
with your devious, sinister ways.
She knows better than to believe you,
when you don't even have
the decency to respect her,
be honest with her.
She knows she doesn't need,
much less,
want you.

Healing

I write these words
because my mind says
I need to heal.
Heal from what?
I am human.
I have feelings.
I cannot "heal" from loving you.
It's simply against the nature
of the vast universe
to unlove you.
I cannot apologize for loving you.
My soul chose you.
I don't need you, and yet,
I want you.
I wish I could grab a vacuum
and suck my pain and sorrow away,
but life doesn't work that way.

I have to let myself go with the flow,
and receive all the blessings
God has in store.
It's a matter of faith and hope,
even if that means
we're never meant to be.

Angel, Rest in Peace

You are my one and only angel.

My heart is fragile,
because it cannot contain my love for you.

You had the heart of an Angel,
and the mind of a Rebel.

My Angel is gone,
and is better off resting her soul.

My beautiful Rebel,
Rest in Peace.

Odyssey of Love • Joseph C. Reyes

Depression

I Was Born

I was born fragile and weak,
mostly because of my disability,
constant struggles with my self-esteem,
always wondering why I'm unhappy,
thinking about what I'm missing,
worrying about what people truly think of me,
riddled by thoughts that haunt me
and a mountain of self-loathing.

Yet, people say I'm unique,
that I'm good and a kind soul.
If only my mind
would let me believe it's so.

Ghosts of The Past

My life is full of blunders,
they make me cry all the time.
I feel hopeless and pathetic
my heart is torn and broken,
my thoughts torture me every night.
I think my mind is tormented,
by the ghosts of the past.

Tonight

Tonight, I write these words
with a heavy heart.
My mind has sunk in horrible thoughts.
I lay in bed with terrible sadness,
my eyes swollen
from pain and unhappiness.
I often wish for a swift death,
but then I step back with hateful regret.
Tonight, I will sleep
with loathing and fears,
hopeful I wake up
with a genuine smile to uncloak.

I Didn't Ask You To...

I didn't ask you to bring me this far.
You feel so pathetic and worthless,
always worrying what others think of you.
Why didn't you give up
when you had the chance?!
The opportunity was right in your hands!
You look in the mirror
and you hate what you see.
You're always complaining,
"Why do people hate me?"
I'm waiting for the day
you come to the realization,
you're only torturing your mind
and straining your genuine connections.
But I'm tired of fighting with you,
or possibly for you.
If you want a happy ending,
you either follow your heart or end it all.

You choose.

Bound by Bones

I'm bound by these bones of pain and sorrow.
The monster of depression
creeps from under my bed,
crying myself to sleep at night.
Horrible thoughts of the past
are inscribed on my brain,
fear of failure flowing through my veins.
But I will not despair,
the day will come where hope prevails.

Incapable

I can't shake these tormenting thoughts,
the desire of going to sleep,
peacefully,
and never waking up.
Never opening my eyes again
to these feelings of being
　　　　　　　useless,
　　　　　　　　　worthless,
　　　　　　　　　　pathetic,
But worst of all,
Incapable
　　　of ever feeling loved.

This feels like the end,
I'm tired of being the main event,
　　　　　　the celebrated guest,
of this pity parade.

Odyssey of Love • Joseph C. Reyes

Odyssey of Love • Joseph C. Reyes

Bilingual Poetry

Llévame

Llévame en tus aposentos
De tú corazón.
Tócame con ternura
y bésame con pasión.
Deja que nuestro amor
germine por noches incontables
y que nunca llegue el día
que tenga que olvidarte,
con tanto dolor.

Take Me

Take me to the deepest corners
of your heart.
Touch me with tenderness
and kiss me with passion.
Let our love blossom
for countless nights,
eluding the day
I'll have to forget you,
with great despair.

Amor Encerrado

Estoy atrapado entre palabras
de amor y desamor,
sin oportunidad de ver
la mirada chispeante en tu ojo
y tú sonrisa que derrite el corazón.
Atrapado por estas paredes enjauladas,
sueño con abrazarte
y sentir tu calor.
Anhelo que me salves
de este amor encerrado
que me ha dejado sin alientoy sin color.

Lockdown Love

I'm stuck between words
of love and heartbreak,
without a chance to see
the sparkling gaze in your eye
and heart-melting smile.
Trapped by these caging walls,
I dream of holding you
and feel your warmth.
I yearn for you to save me
from this lockdown love
that's left me breathless and pale.

Èchame La Culpa

Échame la culpa
por todos los errores que he cometido.
Échame la culpa
por no haber estado contigo
cuando me necesitabas.
Échame la culpa
por no haberte dado
todo el amor y respeto
que tanto te mereces.
Nunca fue mi intención
causarte dolor y tristeza.

Ahora que ya no estamos juntos,
Échame la culpa
pero de rodillas,
imploro,
perdóname.

Blame Me

Blame me
for all the mistakes I've made.
Blame me
for not being there for you
when you needed me.
Blame me
for not giving you all the love and respect,
you deserve so much.
It was never my intention
to cause you pain and sadness.

Now that we're not together,
Blame me
but,
on my knees I beg,
forgive me.

Girasol

Brillando cómo la luz del sol,
tu sonrisa resplandece
lo más recóndito de mi ser.
Mi alma se regocija
al encontrarme con tu mirada,
escapándome de la oscuridad
de mi corazón.
El calor de tu piel
despierta el amor que encuentras en mi,
siendo el girasol que sale
reluciendo al amanecer.
Felicidad he encontrado contigo,
sintiéndome seguro
en la fuerza de tus brazos,
aún después de la puesta del sol.

Sunflower

Shining like the light of the sun,
your smile brightens the deepest,
hidden parts of my being.
My soul rejoices with your gaze,
escaping from the darkness of my heart.
The warmth of your skin
awakens the love within me,
having to be the sunflower
glittering at the break of dawn.
Happiness I have found with you,
Feeling safe in the strength
of your arms even after
the sun's setting.

Rosas de Amor

Un pareado de versos románticos,
Un par de rosas marchitándose,
atormentadas por el dolor de sus espinas,
pero en vigor al fin
por un amor destinado a durar
en interminables noches de pasión.

Roses of Love

A couplet of romantic verses,
A pair of wilting roses
tormented by their painful thorns,
but in vigor at last
by a love meant to last
in endless nights of passion.

Sombra de Amor

Tú sonrisa resplandeciente
y el brillo de tus ojos
me convenció que nuestras almas
estaban unidas,
nuestro amor era real e infinito.
Encontraste mi alma
fríamente oscura,
pero un beso tuyo
era todo lo que necesité
para convertirme en tu eterno luz solar.
Bajo el refugio de tus calurosos brazos,
nunca rehusaré
de resguardarme bajo tu sombra
de amor.

Shade of Love

Your radiant smile
and your glowing eyes
convinced me that our souls
were connected,
our love was real and infinite.
You found my soul
cold in the darkness,
but a kiss from you
was all I needed
to become your eternal sunshine.
Under the refuge of your warm arms,
I will never refuse to seek protection
under your shade
of love.

Estrellas fugaces

Tus ojos brillan como
hermosas estrellas fugaces,
iluminando mi mundo
de soledad con tu amor.
Tus brazos me brindan el calor
para poder sobrevivir este mundo
de corazón frío y cruel.
Mi vida pertenece
única y exclusivamente a ti,
porque tú solamente tienes el poder
de demoler las paredes
que resguardan este corazón.
Cúbreme con la sombra de tu amor,
y siempre seré tu luna guiadora

Falling stars

Your eyes shine
like beautiful falling stars,
illuminating my world
of loneliness with your love.
Your arms provide
the warmth I need
to survive this cold hearted, cruel world.
My life belongs only and exclusively to you,
for you have the power
to tear down the walls that guard this heart.
Cover me with the shadow of your love,
and I will forever be your guiding moon.

Amor de Madre

No se donde estaría sin mi vida con ella,
las lecciones de mi madre
han sido las más valorables.
Desde los días de mi pequeñez
hasta los años de mi vejez,
sus palabras seguirán dejando
huella en mi corazón.
Cuando me advertía
que tenga cuidado al cruzar la calle,
hasta cuándo me prohibía
comer tanto chocolate,
esos son los momentos
que ahora me causan risa.
Aunque en mi vida
he tenido muchos contratiempos,
siempre me alegra el alma
el amor de madre que disfruto día a día.

A Mother's Love

I don't know where my life
would be without her,
the lessons of my mother
have been the most valuable.
From the days of my childhood to
the years of my old age,
her words will keep leaving a mark in my heart.
When she warned me to be careful
when crossing the street,
to the times she would forbid me
from eating too many sweets,
these are the moments
that now just make me laugh.
Though in my life
I have had many complications,
my mother's love always
make my soul happy,
day by day.

Renacido

En un mundo como este,
tus labios fueron un dulce licor,
refrescando cada órgano de mi interior.
Tu amor me trajo nueva vida,
renaciendo en el refugio
que encontrè ser tu corazón.
Sin ti, me siento tan perdido;
vacío y seco como la tierra sin lluvia,
que no deja florecer nuestro amor,
bajo la luz del sol y el brillo de la luna.
Nunca dejes de quererme,
mi corazón será tu hogar para siempre.

Reborn

In a world like this,
your lips were a sweet liquor,
refreshing every organ in my interior.
Your love brought me new life,
Being reborn in the refuge
I found to be your heart.
Without you I feel so lost;
empty and dry like earth without rain,
that doesn't let our love bloom
under the brightness of the sun
and the sparkle of the moon.
Never stop your love for me,
my heart, your home will forever be.

Fortaleza

No caben palabras
para describir el amor
qué hay en mi,
Por una mujer tan increíble
desde el día
en que la conocí.
Sabes lo mucho
que pienso en ti,
la diosa que alabo
bajo las estrellas de la noche
y la luz del sol.
Sobre un pedestal
te he colocado,
mis pensamientos viajan
en las nubes mas altas
por tu belleza.
Mi amor nunca fallará
bajo la fortaleza de tu alma
e incomparable corazón.

Stronghold

There are no words
to describe the love
that is in me,
For such an incredible woman,
since the day
our eyes came to meet.
You know how much
I think of you,
the goddess that I praise
under the night stars
and the shining sun.
On a pedestal
I have placed you,
my thoughts travel
on the highest clouds
for your beauty.
My love will never falter
under the stronghold of your soul
and heart without compare.

Odyssey of Love • Joseph C. Reyes

Note to Readers

I am so grateful to my friends and family
for supporting me in the production of this
book. In your hands, you hold a piece of my
heart, a part of my story, a part of who I am.
I have opened the doors to personal experiences
and feelings we all have felt at some point.
My hope is you can find a little light in this
dark world and make a little home in your
heart for my words.

Printed in Great Britain
by Amazon